ART DECO

ART DECO

VICTOR ARWAS

ACADEMY EDITIONS · LONDON
ST. MARTIN'S PRESS · NEW YORK

ACKNOWLEDGEMENTS

With the exception of contemporary documents, all items illustrated come from the collection of the author or from Editions Graphiques Gallery.

Opposite: Louis Icart — *Fumée,* etching in colour, 1926
Frontispiece: Ceramic plate by Cardinal with a design by Georges Lepape

First published in Great Britain in 1976 by
Academy Editions 7 Holland Street London W8

SBN 85670 224 2

First published in the U.S.A. in 1976 by
St. Martin's Press Inc.
175 Fifth Avenue New York NY 10010

Library of Congress Catalog Card Number 76-44579

Printed and bound in Great Britain by
Cox & Wyman Ltd, Fakenham

Art Deco is a useful term which has come to be accepted fairly universally to cover the multitude of decorative styles which proliferated in the years between the two World Wars. But while it is helpful to have such a portmanteau term, a certain confusion has arisen because "Art Deco" is equally widely used as a term to cover a particular style which came to its apogee in the 1925 Paris International Exhibition of Modern Decorative and Industrial Arts, whose abbreviated French title "Les Arts Décos" (short for L'Exposition Internationale des Arts Décoratifs et Industriels Modernes) is the basis for the term. For the sake of clarity, I therefore propose to use Arts Décos in the plural to mean this style, perversely retaining the singular Art Deco to cover the spectrum of styles of the period.

Art Deco is frequently thought of as a reaction by some younger designers against the floral excesses of Art Nouveau, which is assumed to have died around 1910. In fact Art Nouveau, though it reached its creative peak in the short years from 1890 to 1905 never imposed itself as a major decorative style in its heyday. Very few buildings were erected in the style. Very few wealthy patrons decorated their homes in the style. Very few collectors avidly accumulated the equally few objects which were created in the style. Very few contemporary critics were capable of appreciating and enjoying the eclectic and highly idiosyncratic creations of the style. It is only when the true creators were either dead or had moved onto different styles that the vulgarisers came in and made the style popular. Emile Gallé died in 1904, but industrially produced Gallé glass made for years thereafter attained its great and lasting popularity in a totally debased form. "Art Nouveau" derivative knick-knacks in painted metal or glass, "Art Nouveau" inspired graphics and

5

designs went on being made until the Second World War. Indeed, after a brief interruption, Art Nouveau floralism is again in common use in various decorative and advertising schemes. English Art Nouveau really only began at the turn of the century, and Liberty Art Nouveau silver and pewter was made continuously until the late 1920s. Tiffany went on producing his superb glass, lamps and other objects until 1928.

The Universal Exhibition of 1900, designed to herald in the new millenium, was built in a curious hodge-podge of styles in which Art Nouveau played only a very tiny part. Contemporary mention of the few Art Nouveau architectural features tend to refer to them as "in the Scottish style." S. Bing displayed a range of objects and pictures in his "Maison de l'Art Nouveau," and several trade and regional pavilions displayed a few original designs. The vast majority were traditional, imitative, historicist, and dull. This was the spur needed to get such original designers as Grasset, Guimard, Decoeur, Follot, Gaillard, Dufrêne, Francis Jourdain and Pierre Chareau to form a new group, the Société des Artistes Décorateurs (The Society of Artist Decorators) in 1901. They were to organise regular Salons in which to display new designs, but their real purpose was to organise a great international exhibition of all that was best in contemporary decorative art. After endless bickering and discussion, the Exhibition was planned for 1915, then postponed to 1916 The outbreak of war in 1914 shelved the project indefinitely, but it was re-

vived after the Armistice in 1918. Replanned for 1922, they decided that 1924 was a more practical date because of the postwar exhaustion. In fact it was to open in April 1925, a quarter of a century after the great Universal Exhibition.

Various "national" styles were, in the meantime, impinging on each other. In Glasgow Charles Rennie Mackintosh had rediscovered the decorative functions of the straight line in both architecture and furniture design. A similar rediscovery was taking place in Austria. The Scot was invited to exhibit at the Vienna Secession in 1900; the impact was enormous. Two years later Josef Hoffmann and Kolo Moser, two of the leading members of the Secession, went to Britain for the First International "Studio" Exhibition. They visited Mackintosh and his friends in Glasgow, as well as Charles Robert Ashbee's Guild of Handicrafts in Poplar. The Guild "Workshop" system of training local craftsmen in a wide range of crafts to produce original designs greatly impressed them. A year later they joined with Fritz Wärndorfer, a banker and art collector, to found the Wiener Werkstätte. This consisted of a group of workshops where craftsmen co-ordinated designs in furniture, leathers, fabrics, carpets, glass, precious and base metals and other crafts as well as with the architecture and interior designs in which these were to be housed. Kolo Moser introduced a basically angular and geometric style which was to remain until 1906, when the Secession movement split and he left with

Advertisement for Panhard cars, 1932

Klimt and his followers. After 1906 the Wiener Werkstätte style tended to become increasingly fanciful and amusingly elaborate in its decoration. Nevertheless Wiener Werkstätte designers in the first few years of the association's existence succeeded in establishing most of the styles later to be considered as Art Deco. Josef Hoffmann, in particular, designed flatware in 1903 which is strikingly similar to that of the modernists of the 1930s. His Palais Stoclet in Brussels, built between 1905 and 1908, incorporates all that is most sumptuous in materials and decoration within a geometric framework in which the succession of straight lines is placed at continually surprising angles to each other to seduce the eye.

In 1907 the German architect Hermann Muthesius founded the Deutscher Werkbund in Munich to bring together artists, artisans and industry to improve industrial design. Josef Hoffmann was again at the forefront, joined by such designers as Henry van de Velde and Richard Riemerschmid. Muthesius firmly believed in standardising design to enable mass production. This eventually brought a split with van de Velde, to whom this meant abdicating the individual role of the artist.

In France, Julius Meier-Graefe, a leading German art critic and editor of the magazine *Pan* had founded the Maison Moderne in 1899 to rival Bing's L'Art Nouveau in offering the finest examples of new designs in *objets d'art* and furniture. Three of its young designers were to move away from Art Nouveau and become leading designers in the Arts Décos style: Paul Follot (1877-1941), Maurice Dufrêne (1876-1955) and Clément Mère. Art Nouveau furniture had failed to achieve wide popularity because it was too revolutionary, too complex. Little nests of tables or single items from the workshops of Gallé or Majorelle fitted into the normal bourgeois home, but for the majority of furniture the choice invariably went to authentic or reproduction 18th Century. The new style was to be an adaptation of 18th Century shapes, simplified at times, but made unique by the use of the rarest woods, often covered in parchment or sharkskin, inlaid with marquetry, ivory, leather panels or laquer.

In 1905 several young painters were grouped together in one of the rooms at the Salon because the hanging supervisor saw a similarity in their violent use of colour. An innocuous traditional statue placed in the same room led a critic to exclaim that it was "Donatello among the wild beasts." The painters had been given the name "Les Fauves" - the wild beasts. Their shocking use of harsh primary colours horrified viewers brought up to admire the muted tones considered to be in good taste. Some designers, however, found these colours inspiring and liberating. The arrival of the Ballets Russes in 1909, with the barbaric splendour of their décors and costumes by Bakst shook these decorators further. The exhibition of designs from the Deutscher Werkbund at the 1910 Salon d'Automne, with their strong lines and deep contrasting colours, provided the final liberating blow.

The great dress designers became the chief patrons of the new styles. Paul Poiret was, by 1910, the leading couturier, having liberated women from their multiple underclothes and corsets. He employed Erté and José de Zamora to draw his clothes. He commissioned Paul Iribe in 1908 and Georges Lepape in 1911 to draw albums commemorating his Collections. In 1911 he set up a small workshop for the printing of fabrics designed by Raoul Dufy. Dufy, who was later to design fabrics for the firm of Bianchini Ferrier, also decorated mirrors and furniture and designed posters in a style very similar to his easel paintings. In 1912 Poiret set up the Martine School, where twelve-year-old girls from working-class backgrounds were taught the rudiments of drawing and painting and then encouraged to draw whatever took their fancy on visits to the zoo, parks or the countryside. Poiret selected from the often charming and naive drawings which turned up several designs which were then made up in his Atelier Martine as designs for carpets, wallpapers, cushions or fabrics. The atelier executed furniture and complete interior designs, frequently opulently eastern in inspiration. Poiret also formed a fine collection of paintings and sculptures by Modigliani, Van Dongen, Dunoyer de Segonzac, Picasso, Matisse, Utrillo and Brancusi.

Jacques Doucet, an older eminent Paris couturier for whom the young Poiret had worked, suddenly sold off his superb collection of 18th Century furniture and objects in 1912 and commissioned Paul Iribe to design his new apartment in the Arts Décos style. In 1928, when over seventy years old, Doucet built himself a superb studio designed by Ruau, with furniture by Pierre Legrain, Marcel Coard, Eileen Gray, André Groult, Rose Adler, Iribe and others, with sculptures and *objets d'art* by Miklos, Csacki and Brancusi. These two commissions represent the two great opposed styles of Art Deco, Arts Décos and Modernism.

Synthetic and analytic cubism as proposed by Braque and Picasso had a limited interest and survival value, but the influence of its surface appearance was enormous. In some form or other it has affected most artists and decorators. Some, like Juan Gris and Jacques Villon, had their creative abilities stunted by it. Others, like the engraver Laboureur, used it to create a new type of figuration which has since become a commonplace. The geometric lines and break up of planes was adapted by furniture and interior designers, sometimes incongruously. Paul Iribe devised his "Cubist rose," which became one of the great decorative motifs which recur throughout the twenties, rivalled only by the floral garland and basket of fruit and flowers devised by Paul Véra. The machine, too brought a new dimension to design. Marinetti's *Futurist Manifesto,* published in 1909, announced that "the splendour of the world has become enriched by a new beauty: the beauty of speed. A racing car with its bonnet wreathed with thick tubes like serpents with explosive breaths ... is more beautiful than the Victory of Samothrace." Indeed, the 20s and 30s was an era of superbly hand-built cars; sleek, aerodynamic, the spirit of the glorious future that was sure to come.

The 1925 Paris International Exhibition of Modern Decorative and Industrial Art was the great and final triumph of the Arts Décos style. Created in the pre-war days of creative ferment, it had revived in the immediate post-war years to fuel the demands of those who had made money during the war. The two high-priests of the opulent style were Emile-Jacques Ruhlmann, who designed and built in his workshops furniture of the most exquisite combinations of rare woods and decorative coverings, generally complemented with paintings and murals by Jean Dupas; and the Compagnie des Arts Français, founded in 1919 by Louis Süe and André Mare to design and build complete interiors. The pavilions they furnished were the supreme examples of their mannered style. But the era of Arts Décos was passing. Süe and Mare closed their doors in 1928. Ruhlmann died in 1933. The day of the Modernists was dawning.

The cubist line, allied to extreme simplification and the rejection of extraneous decoration, became the credo of several artists. Some, like the architect

Rene Vincent — *L'heure du bain,* watercolour

Robert Mallet-Stevens, the sculptors Joel and Jan Martel, were more fascinated by the machine itself than by its possibilities.

Le Corbusier and Amedée Ozenfant launched their "Purist" movement in 1918 as a rationalisation of Cubism, aiming for "the purging of the plastic vocabulary by sweeping out parasite words." Two years later they launched a magazine, *L'Esprit Nouveau* (The New Spirit). Le Corbusier wrote "A house is a machine for living in." His ideas were concretely exposed in the 1925 Exhibition in the L'Esprit Nouveau pavilion. Built of concrete, steel and glass, the stark interior had a minimum of simple furniture, white walls with only a very few cubist paintings hanging, and a split level use of space. It had been built in a far corner of the Exhibition grounds, and the Fine Arts Ministry had to intervene at the last minute to order the removal of hoardings which the horrified director of the Exhibition had had put up to conceal the building. In 1930 Le Corbusier, Mallet-Stevens, Djo-Bourgeois and Eileen Gray joined

Le Corbusier and Pierre Jeanneret — Villa in Boulogne-Sur-Seine

the new Union des Artistes Modernes, founded by René Herbst. They were dedicated to the rejection of all unnecessary ornamentation, the use of new materials, steel, chromium, painted metal and the devising of mass produced furniture and sectional elements. When, however, Le Corbusier, his cousin Pierre Jeanneret and Charlotte Perriand presented their first range of modern furniture, edited by the Austrian firm of Thonet, it was a curious adaptation of that firm's traditional furniture, with the bentwood replaced by chrome-plated metal tubes and woven straw replaced by hide.   Yet this was to be the new dominant style. Known after the name of their group as "Modernism," or more commonly in the United States as "Art Moderne," this was the second major strand of Art Deco, characterised by simplification, chunky shapes, straight lines, white walls and pure geometric inspirations. This was the decorative art of the thirties.

Erté, Iribe and others had gone to the United States and had carried their decorative ideas to Hollywood and Broadway. Modernism was also quickly adopted by Hollywood, which used some of its decorative ideas in curious conjunctions with sumptuous looking materials to create the dream-world interiors which the movies were to set up as the epitome of wealth. The occasional Lubitsch film had the truly simplified Modernist interiors, but most were in the newly developing derivative Kitsch style.

Extraordinary buildings were springing up in New York, Chicago and San Francisco. Their architects were not worried by the struggle between the Arts Décos style and Modernism; they frequently incorporated aspects of both

Le Corbusier and Pierre Jeanneret — *L'Esprit Nouveau* pavilion at the 1925 Paris Exhibition

to create a new synthetic Art Deco. The perfect example is the Rockefeller Center complex, with its conjunction of different styles of architecture and decoration, and its crowning jewel, the Radio City Music Hall, where both interior and furniture were designed by Donald Deskey. Art Deco also developed in the design and decoration of cars, aeroplanes, refrigerators, bridges, houses and gardens.

It is, however, in the realm of collectible objects that Art Deco proved supreme. Jean Dunand and Eileen Gray executed superb work in true laquer, both having studied the techniques evolved by Japanese artists.

Dunand, Paul-Louis Mergier and Claudius Linossier also executed enamelled vases and boxes, as well as dinanderie work, which involved hammering the metal, usually copper,then decorating it with various acid baths which coloured and discoloured the metal, and overlaying thin layers of silver, gold, nickel and other metals onto the basic body. Fauré and Marty developed at Limoges the technique of building up layers of thick enamelling to form floral and geometric designs onto copper vases.

The most original of the Art Deco silversmiths was Jean Puiforcat, whose supreme elegance of form in design was largely due to the daring way he balanced volumes in space. Gérard Sandoz, George Jensen, Christian Fjerdingstad, Charles Boyton and Gio Ponti were other leading designers.

The inter-war years saw a proliferation of metal workers in wrought iron, bronze and steel. They produced decorative gates, lift shafts, doors, radiator covers, lamp-shades and furniture. Edgar Brandt is the best known, but

Dartey — Fashion drawing for Madeleine Vionnet

Raymond Subes, Edouard Schenck, Schwartz-Haumont, Delion and Nics Frères were other leading designers or manufacturers.

Two opposed tendencies appeared in ceramics. On the one hand men like Decoeur, Lenoble and Delaherche sought to simplify shapes and experimented with glazes to produce an often attractive version of Chinese, Korean or Japanese stoneware. On the other, artists like René Buthaud, André Methey, Raoul Lachenal, Jean Besnard and Jean Mayodon decorated the vases, bowls, and plates they made with splendid figurative or abstract designs that are sometimes of Hellenic or Etruscan inspiration.

It was a highly creative period for glass. Maurice Marinot, one of the original Fauve painters, having gone through a period of learning during which he produced enamelled glass vessels, developed techniques of furnace-worked glass which produced extraordinary effects. Using multiple layers of glass with air bubbles, streams and washes of colour trapped within the layers, he would shape, cut and deep-carve the glass with successive prolonged acid baths. Marinot vases are extremely rare and sought after by collectors. He ha a few disciples such as Henri Navarre and André Thuret while Daum Frères at Nancy and Schneider both produced simplified designs in the Marinot style. Pâte-de-verre (with its variant pâte-de-cristal), produced by the action of slow heat for extended periods on a mould containing a paste of crushed glass, metallic oxides and a catalyst, enabled Gabriel Argy-Rousseau, Decorchemont and Walter to produce brilliant designs, extraordinary colours and dazzling luminosity. Yet there is no doubt that the glass of the period was dominated by Lalique.

Drawing by André Mare cut on wood by A. Chapon

René Lalique, the leading Art Nouveau jeweller, had frequently used glass in his designs. A commission for the perfumer François Coty in 1907 led Lalique to abandon jewellery and concentrate on glass, and he was soon running two factories. It may be worth noting that when he purchased his major factory in 1918, ready to launch himself into the world of glass, he was fifty-eight years old. Using every modern industrial technique he produced an unending series of original designs made in pressed and moulded glass, occasionally using coloured, opalescent or surface-coloured glass. Similar moulded glass was produced by Sabino and Etling in France, and was essayed in Bohemia, Britain and elsewhere. In Sweden, Simon Gate and Edward Hald created for

Réne Lalique — glass radiator caps, *Libellule, Tête de Belier* and *Tete d'Aigle*

Orrefors a range of wheel-engraved and multi-layered glass in Functionalist and other styles. In the Netherlands Functionalism triumphed at the Leerdam glassworks, while Capellin, Venini and Barovier brought a renaissance to Venetian glass.

Remarkable changes took place in the design of jewellery. Geometric shapes, the use of white metals (platinum, white gold and silver) in conjunction with black onyx and diamonds, and the rejection of excess ornamentation all went into creating a new concept of luxury and chic. Baroque, richly encrusted designs were made by Cartier, Van Cleef et Arpels, Dusausoy, Mauboussin and Chaumet. Georges Fouquet, who had designed superb Art Nouveau jewellery produced equally creative models in the Arts Décos style, while his son, Jean Fouquet was considerably more uncompromisingly geometric. Raymond Templier was one of the leading geometricists, closely followed by Gérard Sandoz who was strongly influenced by the look of the machine.

The art of bookbinding was transformed in the inter-war years by Pierre Legrain, who began to use such unusual materials as ivory, wood, mother-of-pearl and sharkskin in conjunction with the finest morocco leathers. Coloured inlays and gold and platinum tooling were also used to accentuate the character of the binding, which was to reflect the book itself. Two great collectors,

Drawing by André Mare cut on wood by A. Chapon

Jacques Doucet in Paris and Major J.R. Abbey in England, were to commission some of the most exquisite twentieth century bindings. Leading designers included Rose Adler, who frequently used snakeskin and laquered leather encrusted with gemstones; F.L. Schmied, who introduced gold and silver as well as laquered panels by Dunand after models by himself and Miklos; and Robert Bonfils, who produced superb contrasts of colour with great sobriety of means. André Mare and F.L. Schmied's son Théo produced original painted parchment bindings.

Art Deco sculpture had many widely diverging styles. The purest, and most striking, is the sculpture of Modigliani, which neatly absorbed the influence of African carvings, and Brancusi, whose smooth, simplified outlines and surfaces created an almost unbearable erotic tension. The great stylisation of these two artists was adopted, adapted and popularised by some artists who formed two conjoined groups called La Stèle and L'Evolution. They included Pierre Le Faguays, Pierre Traverse, Raoul Lamourdedieu and Sibylle May. The two currents of cubism and African carving joined to influence three sculptors, Gustave Miklos, Csaky and Jean Lambert-Rucki. Animalier sculpture abandoned its nineteenth century naturalism in favour of sleek and streamlined stylisations. Here the great master was François Pompom, while Armand

Zeppelins

Petersen, Maurice Prost and Franz Barwig worked in a similar vein. Paul Jouve, Sandoz and Rembrandt Bugatti, on the other hand, used stylisation of shape and attitude with a kneaded surface to capture the essence of the animal, a kind of snapshot effect. Bugatti, who committed suicide in 1916, was the son of Carlo Bugatti, who designed extraordinary wood, parchment and metal furniture of Moorish derivation and geometric lines; and the brother of Ettore Bugatti, designer and builder of one of the most famous racing cars of the inter-war years.

The inter-war years also saw the great popularity of chryselephantine figures, statuettes in which bronze, gold painted or patinated, was combined with carved and often painted ivory to create stylised figures of dancers, nudes, and animals. The multimedia effect was completed with elaborate marble or onyx bases. The two leading artists here were F. Preiss, an Austrian, and Dimitri Chiparus, a Rumanian who worked in Paris. Others include Bouraine, Godard and Le Faguays from France, Colinet from Belgium, Bruno Zach and Roland Paris from Germany, Philippe and Lorenzl from Austria, and Alexandre Kelety from Hungary.

The popularisation of the Art Deco styles took place not in the annual Salons which had opened their doors to the decorative arts, but in the great department stores in Paris. Each of the major stores opened a design studio for the creation and sale of furniture and objects in the new style. Some, indeed, offered a complete interior design service. The Galeries Lafayette opened its design studio under the artistic direction of Maurice Dufrêne in 1921, calling it "La Maitrise." The Printemps store opened "Primavera" under René Guilleré. This is the only design studio, under a succession of directors, to have survived to this day. Au Bon Marché opened "Pomone" under Paul Follot in 1923; while the Grands Magazins du Louvre opened "Studium" under Kohlmann, Djo Bourgeois and Max Vibert.

The great inter-war fashion designers reigned supreme in ordaining the way women dressed as well as in leading the way in decoration. Madeleine Vionnet had her home entirely decorated in laquer ware by Dunand, including a laquer portrait of herself over the mantelpiece. Jeanne Lanvin had both her house and Salon decorated by the sculptor Armand-Albert Rateau, with sculptured furniture and doors. The extravagant Paul Poiret celebrated the 1925 Exhibition by commissioning the decoration of three barges moored on the Seine, which he named Amours, Délices and Orgues (Loves, Delights and Organs). Decorated by his own firm of Martine, which had earlier introduced the sunken bathtub and the home bar, the first barge was set up as a luxurious home, the second as a luxurious restaurant, and the third, fitted with fourteen large mural hangings painted by Raoul Dufy, was the setting for his latest collections. Extravagant and generous with his last penny, Poiret was soon bankrupted and, although his fortunes appeared to revive from time to time, he eventually died destitute.

As fashions changed, fashion magazines arose to inform and illustrate.

Superb illustrators were attracted to fashion, turning the depiction of individual dresses to stylised decorative creations in their own right. Publications such as *La Gazette du Bon Ton* (1912 to 1925), *Modes et Manières d'Aujourd'hui* (1912 to 1922) and others commissioned such artists as Georges Lepape, André Marty, Guy Arnoux, Benito, Erté, Iribe, Barbier, Bonfils, Brunelleschi, Leyritz, Ranson, Zamora, Zig, Zinoviev and Dufy to capture both dresses and interiors. These illustrators also designed décors and costumes for music hall and theatre. The vastly increased use of photography to reproduce clothes reduced the role of the illustrator, though Vogue, Harper's Bazaar and other magazines devoted to fashion have continued to use some illustrators. Poiret, ever the innovator, was the first fashion designer to employ a photographer to capture an entire collection. It was in 1922 and, with his usual flair, he chose the young Man Ray, who developed his rayograph process while working for Poiret.

The vulgarisation of Art Deco styles through derivative ill-made artifacts led to the wholesale condemnation of the original works as well as their kitschy excrescences. This attitude was further complicated by the nightmarish aspects of the Depression which spread over the world from 1929 onwards, followed by a hideously destructive war. It is only now that the gap of years enables us to look at the creations of the period untainted by such associations. Indeed, even the kitsch has served a useful purpose in accustoming our eyes to the basic outlines, allowing us to ignore mere novelty and look at the solid basis of craft and art inherent in the best designs of the period.

Opposite Delatte — reticulated glass and wrought iron lamp

Le Verre Français — lamp, wrought iron base and cameo glass shade

Paul Iribe — bronze lamp

Raymond Subes — wrought iron gate for the Ecole des Arts Décoratifs, Paris

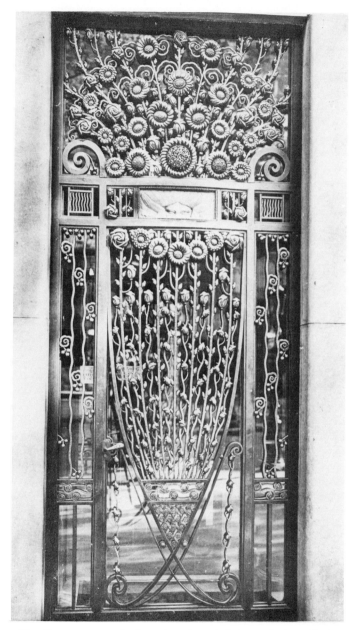

Nics Freres — wrought iron door for a hairdresser's shop, Paris

Edgar Brandt — wrought iron and bronze entrance for the Paris offices of *L'Illustration*

Edgar Brandt — wrought iron and bronze entrance for Paul Poiret's
Paris Salon

Opposite
Edgar Brandt — wrought iron and bronze doors for the Montreal Chamber of Commerce

Above
Bronze and silver plaques by Pierre Turin, P.M. Dammann, F. Delannoy, André Lavrillier, Jean Vernon and Marcel Renard

Maurice Dufrêne — silver and ivory hand mirror

Georg Jensen — silver cocktail shaker, 1929

Charles Boyton — silver and ivory bowl, 1934

Jean Puiforcat — silver lamp and silver and silver-gilt chalice

Gennarelli — silvered bronze statue on marble column

Lorenzl — gilt bronze on onyx base

Bruno Zach — bronze figure

Fayral — silvered bronze

Maurice Guiraud-Riviere — green patinated bronze

Pierre Le Faguays — Bronze. The artist was a member of the *La Stèle* and *L'Evolution Artistique* groups.

Pierre Traverse — Bronze. The artist was a member of the *La Stèle* and *L'Evolution Artistique* groups.

Above
John Duncan Fergusson — Torso, bronze, 1918

Opposite
Gustave Miklos — bronze

44

Opposite
Jöel & Jan Martel — bronze lettering

Above
Jöel & Jan Martel — *Le Lion de Belfort,* zinc sculpture for the Belfort Post Office

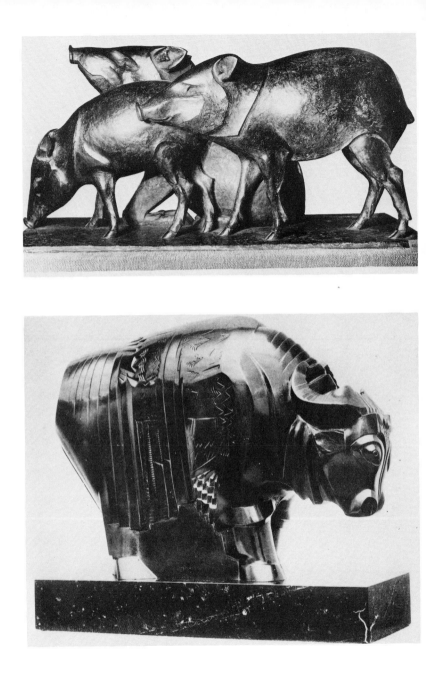

Opposite above
Edouard-Marcel Sandoz — *Peccaries,* bronze

Opposite below
Gustave Miklos — *Bison,* bronze

Above
Wanda — *L'Assaut,* silvered bronze

THE COLOUR PLATES

1 Robert Bonfils — inlaid and gilt morocco binding for *Manon Lescaut* executed in 1931 for Captain J.R. Abbey

2 Jean Dunand — *Les Amants,* lacquer panel

3 Gabriel Argy-Rousseau — *pâte-de-cristal* vases

4 Jewellery in gold, platinum, diamonds, onyx, coral and jade by Lacloche, Georges Fouquet, Boucheron and Templier

5 Jewellery in gold, platinum, rubies etc. by Cartier, Mauboussin and Georges Fouquet

6 Sacha Zaliouk — *Un Couple,* gouache

7 François-Emile Decorchemont — green *pâte-de-verre* vase

8 F. Preiss — clock, carved ivory, onyx and marble

English silver cigarette box with enamelled lid, 1914

P. Mergier — *Diane,* dinanderie vase, stained, etched and hammered pewter

Fauré — enamel vase on copper

René Lalique — brown glass vase with bison handles

René Lalique — *Sauterelles,* glass vase with blue and green staining

René Lalique — *Poissons,* glass vase with green staining

René Lalique — *Chardons,* glass vase with orange staining

Opposite
René Lalique — glass flacon modelled in relief

Above
René Lalique — *Serpents,* glass lamp

René Lalique — reddish brown glass vase

René Lalique — zig zag shaped glass vase decorated with birds

Above
Orrefors — glass vase designed by Simon Gate

Opposite
Daum — blue cameo glass bowls, deep acid etching

Above
Jean Luce — intaglio-cut mirrored and frosted glass vase

Opposite
Simonet Frères — bronze, glass and quartz standard lamp, designed by
Albert Simonet and Henri Dieupart

71

Above
Maurice Marinot — furnace worked and deeply acid cut glass vases

Below
René Buthaud — enamel decorated stoneware vases and bowl

Jean Mayodon — enamel decorated stoneware vase in green and gold

Above
Keith Murray — ceramic vase for Wedgwood

Opposite
Ceramic lamp by Sybille May decorated in enamels by Cazaux. Both artists
were members of the *La Stèle* and *L'Evolution Artistique* groups.

Pendants and brooches by Raymond Templier, Dusausoy, Georges Fouquet, Linzeler & Marchak, Vever, Gérard Sandoz and Lacloche, necklace by Boucheron

Pendants by Dusausoy, Chaumet, Georges Fouquet and Gérard Sandoz, brooches by Aucoc and Mauboussin, bracelet by G. Fouquet

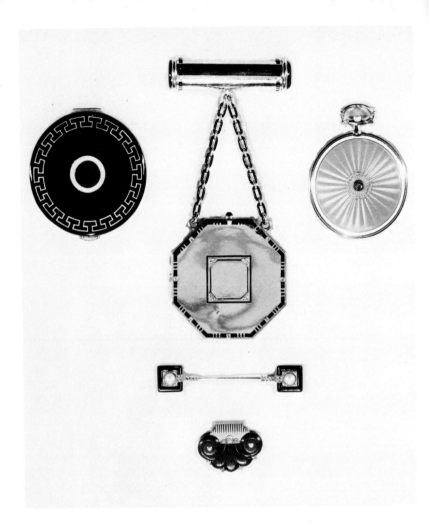

Above
Cartier — compact, minaudière, watch, brooch and clip in gold, enamel and diamonds

Opposite
Carved amber and ebony cigarette holders

Above
Fashion drawing by Garcia Benito

Opposite
Fashion drawing for a cape

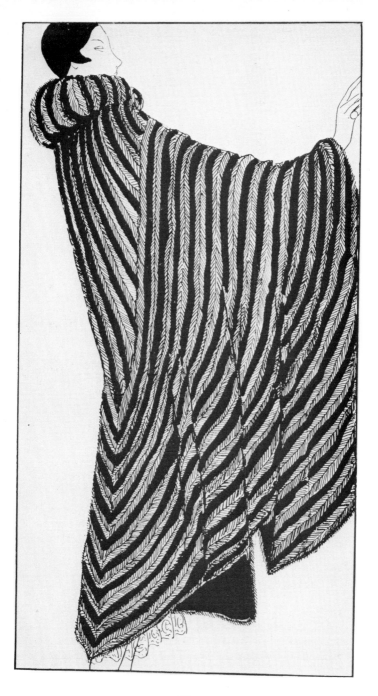

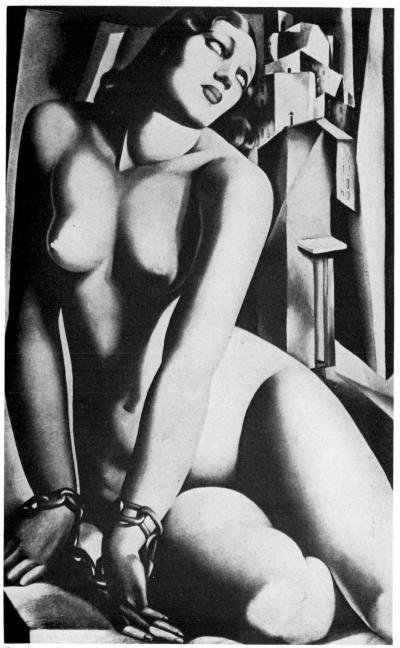

Opposite above
Jean Dupas — *Toreau,* charcoal and coloured crayon drawing, 1928

Opposite below Eric George — *The Martyrdom of St. Sebastian,* oil, 1925

Above Tamara de Lempicka, *Andromeda,* oil

Louis Icart — *Parfum de Fleurs,* etching in colour, 1937

Opposite
Norman Hartnell — *The Secret,* gouache and watercolour

Above
Leo Rauth — *Fascination Valse,* pochoir in colour

Georges Barbier — *La Danseuse aux Jets d'Eau,* watercolour & gouache, 1925